I0429213

U.S.–RUSSIA NUCLEAR ARMS NEGOTIATIONS: UKRAINE AND BEYOND

JOINT HEARING

BEFORE THE

SUBCOMMITTEE ON TERRORISM, NONPROLIFERATION, AND TRADE

AND THE

SUBCOMMITTEE ON EUROPE, EURASIA, AND EMERGING THREATS

OF THE

COMMITTEE ON FOREIGN AFFAIRS HOUSE OF REPRESENTATIVES

ONE HUNDRED THIRTEENTH CONGRESS

SECOND SESSION

APRIL 29, 2014

Serial No. 113–150

Printed for the use of the Committee on Foreign Affairs

Available via the World Wide Web: http://www.foreignaffairs.house.gov/ or http://www.gpo.gov/fdsys/

U.S. GOVERNMENT PRINTING OFFICE

87–711PDF   WASHINGTON : 2014

For sale by the Superintendent of Documents, U.S. Government Printing Office
Internet: bookstore.gpo.gov   Phone: toll free (866) 512–1800; DC area (202) 512–1800
Fax: (202) 512–2104   Mail: Stop IDCC, Washington, DC 20402–0001

COMMITTEE ON FOREIGN AFFAIRS

EDWARD R. ROYCE, California, *Chairman*

CHRISTOPHER H. SMITH, New Jersey
ILEANA ROS-LEHTINEN, Florida
DANA ROHRABACHER, California
STEVE CHABOT, Ohio
JOE WILSON, South Carolina
MICHAEL T. McCAUL, Texas
TED POE, Texas
MATT SALMON, Arizona
TOM MARINO, Pennsylvania
JEFF DUNCAN, South Carolina
ADAM KINZINGER, Illinois
MO BROOKS, Alabama
TOM COTTON, Arkansas
PAUL COOK, California
GEORGE HOLDING, North Carolina
RANDY K. WEBER SR., Texas
SCOTT PERRY, Pennsylvania
STEVE STOCKMAN, Texas
RON DeSANTIS, Florida
DOUG COLLINS, Georgia
MARK MEADOWS, North Carolina
TED S. YOHO, Florida
LUKE MESSER, Indiana

ELIOT L. ENGEL, New York
ENI F.H. FALEOMAVAEGA, American
  Samoa
BRAD SHERMAN, California
GREGORY W. MEEKS, New York
ALBIO SIRES, New Jersey
GERALD E. CONNOLLY, Virginia
THEODORE E. DEUTCH, Florida
BRIAN HIGGINS, New York
KAREN BASS, California
WILLIAM KEATING, Massachusetts
DAVID CICILLINE, Rhode Island
ALAN GRAYSON, Florida
JUAN VARGAS, California
BRADLEY S. SCHNEIDER, Illinois
JOSEPH P. KENNEDY III, Massachusetts
AMI BERA, California
ALAN S. LOWENTHAL, California
GRACE MENG, New York
LOIS FRANKEL, Florida
TULSI GABBARD, Hawaii
JOAQUIN CASTRO, Texas

AMY PORTER, *Chief of Staff*   THOMAS SHEEHY, *Staff Director*
JASON STEINBAUM, *Democratic Staff Director*

CONTENTS

U.S.–RUSSIA NUCLEAR ARMS NEGOTIATIONS: UKRAINE AND BEYOND

TUESDAY, APRIL 29, 2014

House of Representatives,
Subcommittee on Terrorism, Nonproliferation, and Trade
AND
Subcommittee on Europe, Eurasia, and Emerging Threats,
Committee on Foreign Affairs,
Washington, DC.

The committees met, pursuant to notice, at 1:30 p.m., in room 2172 Rayburn House Office Building, Hon. Ted Poe (chairman of the subcommittee) presiding.

Mr. POE. Subcommittees will come to order and without objection all members may have 5 days to submit statements, questions, and extraneous materials for the record and subject to the length of limitation in the rules.

In a matter of weeks, Putin and his commandos stole Crimea. Now he is on to Eastern Ukraine. I and other Members of Congress were in Ukraine last week and the people were rightfully concerned about Putin's next move into their nation.

According to press reports this morning, Secretary Kerry said that we now have intelligence revealing that operatives in Ukraine are taking orders directly from Moscow. Secretary Kerry also said that some of the same Russian operatives from Crimea and Georgia have shown up in Eastern Ukraine.

When I went to Eastern Ukraine one of the officials gave me a wanted poster for what he called Russian saboteurs. It is in Ukrainian and he—it is on the screen, I hope it is up—this is a copy of the wanted poster and he was willing to pay out of his own money for Russian equipment that had been—it was confiscated by Ukrainians, everything from machine guns, rifles. To anybody that is occupying one of the Ukrainian buildings without permission he is willing to offer rewards for that.

So I thought that was quite interesting that they are concerned about the insurrection or insurgence in his own part of the state.

I believe these actions should—we should understand that we have to reevaluate our agreements with the Russians because of their failure to abide by international law in that they have entered Crimea, Ukraine and even other Baltic states are concerned and so reflected that in conversations with them.

In my opinion, the Russians are not our allies. They are not our friends and we certainly can't take them for their word. Exhibit A is the Intermediate Range Nuclear Forces Treaty, the INF, and this treaty between the United States and Russia places limits on ground-launched ballistic and cruise missiles with ranges between 500 and 5,500 kilometers.

The United States has held up our agreement in the treaty. It appears the Russians have not. According to press reports, it appears the Russians have tested a ground-launched cruise missile from an operational launcher. The Russians have responded this is a sea-based missile, which does not fall under the treaty.

There is no way to know if it is a sea-based missile until it is actually deployed. But even so, if it was a sea-based missile and the Russians tested it on land using an operational launcher it is violation of the treaty.

Either way, the Russians are violating this treaty. According to press reports, the administration knew about the violation back in 2008. Six years later, the State Department says the violation is still under review and has not officially classified it as a violation or not. Time for the State Department to pick a horse and ride it. Either it is a violation or it is not a violation.

I have introduced H. Con. Res. 94 with Representative Rogers and Joe Heck, calling the Russians out for their violation and the administration for its refusal to tell it like it is.

We had hoped that a formal determination would be in this year's arms control compliance report but the report itself due in April is already late.

Apparently, the State Department needs more time to figure out what the rest of us already believe. The Russians do not have to worry about violations as much as the New START treaty. During negotiations, they gutted the verifications that were in the old START treaty.

The most significant changes were the elimination of verification measures for some ICBMs and reduction of total number of inspections. When the Senate was debating approval in 2010, critics argued the treaty was nonsensical because the Russians were already at or below the required levels in key categories while we had delivery vehicles and warheads that were way above these new levels.

Just like the critics warned, the Russians have since undergone the most extensive nuclear modernization since the end of the Cold War, all without violating the New START treaty. We had a reason to be distrustful of the Russians when the New START went into effect in 2010 and we have more reasons today.

The fact is Russia is willing to treat these treaties as less than binding when it suits them. That is not how treaties are supposed to work. Despite this, the administration has pledged to seek deeper cuts in nuclear arms.

In June 2013, the President called for the reduction of our deployed strategic nuclear weapons by up to one-third. My personal opinion is this would be dangerous and is misguided, based on the information that we have about the Russians.

Fortunately, Putin may have saved us from ourselves. The Russians have ''no apparent interest in further arms reductions before 2017,'' according to numerous arms control experts.

The United States should not continue to seek agreements with the Russians when they either cheat or show no interest in those agreements. I don't think—it is not now the time to be kowtowing to Putin, and I will now turn to the ranking member from California for his opening statement, Mr. Sherman, for 5 minutes.

Mr. SHERMAN. I yield to the gentleman from Massachusetts.

Mr. POE. The gentleman from Massachusetts, Mr. Keating, is recognized for 5 minutes.

Mr. KEATING. I thank Mr. Sherman for allowing me to attend a meeting where my presence is required for a quorum and I thank Chairman Poe and Chairman Rohrabacher for convening this important hearing.

I would like to begin thanking Ms. Friedt and Mr. Hartley for appearing today. Both witnesses have extensive experience on Russia and on European security interests. I am looking forward to hearing their assessment of the long-term strategic implication of Russia's illegal invasion of Crimea, its subsequent efforts to destabilize Ukraine's interim government and other matters.

Despite its April 17th pledge to help de-escalate the crisis in Ukraine, Russia has done exactly the opposite. The role that Russian special forces have played in destabilizing Eastern Ukraine is indisputable in supporting so-called separatist-coordinated armed attacks on government buildings and on orchestrating kidnaps and violence against local politicians, reporters and even OSCE monitors.

Russian disinformation campaigns have only made matters worse. Russian forces use the masked warfare and other covert tactics seen to signal a strategic shift in its approach to the region and to European security.

It is essential that the United States and NATO allies respond. I welcome the administration's decision yesterday to impose a third round of sanctions on individuals and entities closely linked to the Russian leadership's inner circle.

I also welcome the decision to impose export restrictions on 13 Russian companies and the additional restrictive measures on defense exports.

The goal of these targeted sanctions is to send a clear signal that Russian aggression against Ukraine comes at a price. I share the President's hope that these measures will persuade President Putin to reverse course.

Unfortunately, I am not optimistic that the steps taken to date will be sufficient. I therefore fully support the administration's readiness to impose additional penalties if Russia continues to press forward including targeted sanctions against specific sectors of the Russian economy.

As the United States moves forward, it is imperative that we do so in a coordinated effort with our European allies. I applaud today's announcement of further EU sanctions on Russia.

I look forward to hearing from Mr. Hartley about the status of the administration's ongoing discussions with the EU as well as plans within NATO to counter Russian aggression and reassure our Central European and Baltic allies.

I also look forward to hearing from Ms. Friedt about the status of existing arms and existing control agreements between the United States and Russia.

4

While further arms control reductions seem unlikely in the current environment, I am relieved that the United States and Russia have continued to implement the New START agreement included by exchanging notifications and conducting on-site inspections.

These exchanges provide much needed stability and predictability at a time of increasing mistrust and uncertainty. I also support the administration's efforts to work through INF treaties' compliance review mechanisms to address concerns that Russian activities may be inconsistent with its treaties obligations.

I strongly supported the administration's decision to cut off defense cooperation with Russia. I have consistently called on our European allies to follow suit and to exercise similar scrutiny with respect to defense exports to Russia. However, when it comes to nuclear security, the stakes are much too high to break off communication.

Continued implementation of our arms control agreements with Russia is essential, especially given the unprecedented and unpredictable nature of the crisis in Ukraine. The last thing we need is another nuclear arms race in Europe. With that, I thank you and yield back.

Mr. POE. Gentleman yields back his time. I now will turn to the chairman of the Europe, Eurasia, and Emerging Threats Subcommittee, Mr. Dana Rohrabacher, from California for 5 minutes.

Mr. ROHRABACHER. Thank you very much, Chairman Poe, for calling this hearing is jointly being held between your Terrorism, Nonproliferation, and Trade Subcommittee and the subcommittee which I chair of Europe, Eurasia, and Emerging Threats.

During the 1980s, I had the honor of working with and for President Ronald Reagan. Through his leadership and strength, the United States brought about the collapse of the Evil Empire—the Soviet Union.

I would add that there are many people who I worked with during that time period who can't seem to get over that the Cold War is over and are still treating the Soviet—the current Russian Government as if it was the Soviet Government.

We are thankful, however, that the world no longer lives in fear of annihilation and no longer lives with a Soviet Union that is controlled by a diabolical philosophy of Marxism, Leninism which motivated people to attempt to put on the world a Marxist, an atheistic dictatorship in the name of perfecting humankind.

We are thankful that that world has been changed and that reality no longer is present and that we no longer live in fear of annihilation between—of a nuclear exchange between those who are motivated by this evil theory—Marxism, Leninism, communism—and the people of the free world.

One of Reagan's greatest accomplishments was negotiating and signing the Intermediate Range Nuclear Forces Treaty, which banned two entire categories of horrific weapons.

I look forward to this hearing today from witnesses about the current efforts to maintain and verify the provisions of that agreement.

I look forward in the future to be discussing with my colleagues some of the fundamental information that they have gleaned from their visits to Ukraine and other places and to have a broader discussion of the nature of the government in Russia today and the threat that it poses or does not pose to the free world as compared to what it was like when I worked for Ronald Reagan in the 1980s.

I also want to speak about another power when we are discussing this issue Mr. Chairman. We should not lose sight that we are not just talking about Russia and the United States.

We are talking about other nuclear weapons in other countries in relationship to what we are doing with the Russians and that is, what is Communist China doing and what are we doing with Russia and other countries that relate to this very issue of strategic weapons with Communist China?

I fear that by continuing to focus our arms control efforts only on Russia while excluding China we are making a grave miscalculation. Our negotiations with Russia dictate our nuclear posture and define our military capabilities.

It should be a major concern that China is not included in these limits including caps set by the New Strategic Arms Limitation Treaty signed in 2010.

Over the past two decades the People's Liberation Army, the armed wing of the Communist Party of China, I might add, has engaged in a massive arms build-up.

Their capability has increased in every area. It is illogical to believe that China's strategic forces and their nuclear stockpile have not also, likewise, been expanded and improved. The United States-China Economic Security Review Commission stated in 2012 the PLA continues to modernize and expand its nuclear stockpile.

China is now on the cusp of obtaining a credible nuclear triad of land-based intercontinental ballistic missiles and submarine-launched ballistic missiles and air-dropped nuclear bombs.

We also know, thanks to the research by Dr. Phillip Karber of Georgetown University, that China has built some 3,000 miles of underground tunnels to store and to transport their nuclear missiles and warheads.

This secret effort by the Chinese military is so massive that it is known as the Underground Great Wall. Beyond this incredible infrastructure, China is also researching hypersonic missiles, ICBMs with maneuvering warheads which then can outmaneuver our defensive systems.

Communist China, in short—and in closing, I would say—Communist China must be included in any discussion of arms control and if we focus only on Russia we are doing a great disservice to the security of our country.

Addressing concerns and priorities with Russia does remain important and the things that are being said today need to be taken into consideration.

Ignoring China's strategic weapons is not an option and will lead us to a much more dangerous world. They must be part of this discussion today and hopefully in the weeks ahead. Thank you, Mr. Chairman.

Mr. POE. The Chair recognizes the ranking member from the Terrorism Subcommittee, Mr. Sherman from California, for 5 minutes.

Mr. SHERMAN. If you watch American television you would think foreign policy is as simple as a cheap Western. Some people are in white hats. Some cowboys are in black hats. If you watch Russian television, you come to the same conclusion only the hat colors have been changed.

If you review what has happened you see that this is far more complicated. A pro-Russian President was elected in legitimate elections in the Ukraine. That legitimately elected President broke his promises, turned his policy on a fundamental issue.

Democratic-elected Presidents have been known to do that. He was swept from power by an insurrection. Those in the insurrection occupied Maidan and it is considered a criminal act to use armed forces—organized government armed forces to dislodge them. Now the government that has taken over in Kiev is using armed government forces to dislodge Eastern Ukrainian occupiers not of Maidan but of various government buildings.

Throughout foreign policy we are faced with the tension between territorial integrity and self-determination. Those were the two greatest wars fought on our own territory—our fight for self-determination from the British and our fight for our territorial integrity and against the self-determination objectives of the confederate states. We look at Crimea as a effort at the self-determination of the Russian-speaking majority there as an illegal act.

We used our Air Force to achieve the independence of Kosovo, which, like the Crimea, was a autonomous region within a republic, which was a relatively newly independent republic, having seceded from a federation—one seceding from the Yugoslav federation, the other seceding from the Soviet Union.

So we have been on both sides of territorial integrity and self-determination both on our own territory in the first 150 years of our existence and in Eastern Europe more recently.

The Russians are interfering in the Eastern Ukraine. Our friends in Kiev are not without fault. They have adopted a change in law that would strip the Russian language of its official status in its southern and eastern provinces.

Fortunately, that law was vetoed. But, clearly, a Parliament, and I should point out a Parliament in which many of the Eastern Ukrainian members felt unsafe and did not attend, would be allowed to pass such a law shows that this is not a government dedicated to reaching out to all of its citizens.

So we have the simplicity of Westerns. We have the reality of foreign policy in Eastern Europe. It is overly simplistic to say that one side is entirely right and one side is entirely wrong just as it is even more simplistic to say that everything would go our way if only we had a President with a different personality.

We had a President with a radically different personality just a decade ago when Georgia lost not one but two of its autonomous regions to Russia, Georgia being smaller, the regions being smaller, the issues being smaller. But you can say what you like about our last two Presidents. The one thing everybody agrees on is they had different personalities.

As to arms control agreements, we have got to trust but verify. Ronald Reagan entered into agreements with a Soviet Union that, clearly, was less trustworthy than Putin is today. Those who enter into these agreements and rely on trust are fooling themselves.

The allegations are twofold. One, that the—that a Russian missile that they call long range was tested at an intermediate range. It seems clear that it is a long range missile.

The other is that a mid-range missile that the Russians say was for sea-based purposes was tested on ground, which is allowed, but tested on ground with what appears to be a operational useable ground-based launcher perhaps one, and I would like to hear from our witnesses, that was mobile. And so it appears as if they were developing a ground-based capacity for this intermediate missile.

Finally, I will point out that four countries have given up their nuclear weapons or their nuclear programs—South Africa, where it worked out well—Saddam, Gaddafi and the Ukraine.

Two of them lost their lives. One of them lost the Crimea. It may be more difficult in the future for us to convince dictators to give up nuclear weapons. It doesn't always work out well. I yield back.

Mr. POE. Without objection, all of the witnesses' prepared statements will be made part of the record and I ask that each witness keep your presentation to no more than 5 minutes.

We are in the middle of votes. We will see how far we can go before we recess for votes and we will resume immediately after the votes. I will introduce both of the witnesses at this time.

Ms. Anita Friedt is the principal deputy assistant secretary for nuclear and strategic policy for the Bureau of Arms Control, Verification and Compliance at the U.S. Department of State.

Ms. Friedt has earned numerous awards including seven superior honor awards for her work on U.S.-Russian European——

Mr. SHERMAN. Mr. Chairman, are other members allowed to give short opening statements?

Mr. POE. All members may have 5 days to submit statements due to the fact that we have votes and we also have two subcommittees. So they can make their comments during their questioning if they wish.

Mr. Brent Hartley is the deputy assistant secretary for the Bureau of European and Eurasian Affairs at the U.S. State Department. Mr. Hartley has extensive experience in European security issues and has served in various roles related to arms control, counterterrorism in NATO and more.

Ms. Friedt, we will start with you. You have 5 minutes.

STATEMENT OF MS. ANITA E. FRIEDT, PRINCIPAL DEPUTY ASSISTANT SECRETARY FOR NUCLEAR AND STRATEGIC POLICY, BUREAU OF ARMS CONTROL, VERIFICATION, AND COMPLIANCE, U.S. DEPARTMENT OF STATE

Ms. FRIEDT. Thank you, Mr. Chairman.

Chairman Poe, Chairman Rohrabacher, Ranking Members Sherman and Keating and members of this committee, I am grateful for the opportunity to speak to you today about the administration's arms control policy toward Russia.

Today, I want to speak to you about three things. One, why arms control agreements with Russia continue to be an important tool to enhance the security of the United States, our allies and partners; two, how we have used arms control tools since the crisis in Ukraine began to increase transparency and stability in support of our broader regional efforts; and three, the seriousness with which the administration takes compliance and arms control treaties.

First, as it has been recognized for over four decades, arms control is a tool that can be used to enhance the security of the United States, our allies and our partners.

The Obama administration has continued the longstanding bipartisan approach to arms control with Russia that had its origins in the days of the Cold War. The administrations of Presidents Ronald Reagan, George W.—and George H.W. Bush were the architects of many of our most successful and enduring arms control efforts.

Let me affirm that the United States is committed to maintaining strategic stability between the United States and Russia and to encouraging mutual steps to foster a more stable, resilient, predictable and transparent security relationship.

That said, Russia's illegal actions in Ukraine have undermined trust. While diplomacy between the United States and Russia continues, no one can ignore that Russia's actions in Ukraine have violated the very principles upon which cooperation is built.

Further, as we consider arms control priorities this year or in any year, we will continue to consult closely with our allies and partners every step of the way. Our security and defense as well as that of our allies and partners is non-negotiable.

We will only pursue arms control agreements that advance our national interest. During the Cold War, Washington and Moscow found it in our mutual interest to work together to tap and then to begin reducing the number of nuclear weapons in service in reversing the nuclear arms race and improving mutual security instability.

We judged that the New START treaty was in the United States' national security interest for the same reasons and that is why we continue to implement the New START treaty with Russia today.

We are now in the fourth year of implementation, and despite the crisis in Ukraine we in Russia continue to implement the treaty in a business-like manner. Since entering into force in 2011 the United States has inspected with boots on the ground Russian nuclear weapons facilities 58 times.

These inspections are as a part of New START's treaty verification regime which is a vital tool in ensuring transparency and predictability between the world's largest nuclear powers.

In the realm of conventional arms control, the United States and our allies have been using arms control mechanisms in an effort to promote stability in Europe, provide transparency in Russia's provocative actions and assure our allies and partners.

I want to underscore that our NATO allies and other partners in Europe strongly support arms control in Europe as well as our active participation and leadership in those efforts.

Since the Ukraine crisis began, the United States and our treaty partners have used the Open Skies treaty to fly 11 missions over Ukraine and western Russia, yielding imagery of thousands of square miles of territory. These flights have resulted in valuable data and insights not only for the United States but our partners and allies as well.

9

We also have confidence-building measures in the Vienna Document to conduct inspections of use and confidence-building measures in Ukraine.

Let me now turn to the issue of compliance. First and foremost, the administration takes compliance with all arms control agreements extremely seriously. For this reason, this administration worked hard to produce a compliance report in 2010, the first compliance report delivered to the Congress since 2005, and we have produced one every year since.

We endeavor every year to produce a compliance report by April 15th. This is admittedly challenging, given the volume of information, the multiple agencies that must comment on it and the seriousness with which the administration conducts its annual compliancereview.

Despite this, we plan to have the report fully coordinated and available later in the spring. As we have previously stated, we have concerns about Russian compliance with the INF treaty.

We have raised them—raised these concerns with Russia and are pressing for clear answers in an effort to resolve these concerns because of the importance of the INF treaty to Euro-Atlantic security.

We have briefed our NATO allies on our concerns and will continue to coordinate with them on this and other matters that affect our common security.

We have kept Congress informed on this matter through briefings with relevant congressional committees and will continue to do so. We will continue to work with Russia to resolve our concerns and to encourage mutual steps to help foster a more stable, resilient, transparent security relationship. We are not going to drop the issue until our concerns have been addressed.

Let me conclude by reiterating our strong belief that arms control treaties and agreements continue to be an important tool that can enhance the security of the United States and our friends and allies.

The successful implementation of the New START treaty and the important contributions that Open Skies treaty and the Vienna Document have played recently in Ukraine demonstrate the continued relevance of arms control for our national security.

Thank you very much. I look forward to your questions.

[The prepared statement of Ms. Friedt follows:]

Testimony of Anita E. Friedt
Acting Assistant Secretary of State
Bureau of Arms Control, Verification and Compliance
Joint Subcommittee Hearing: U.S.-Russia Nuclear Arms Negotiations:
Ukraine and Beyond
April 29, 2014, House Foreign Affairs Committee

Chairmen Poe and Rohrabacher, Ranking Members Sherman and Keating, and members of this Committee, I am grateful for the opportunity to speak to you about the Administration's arms control policy toward Russia.

Today, I want to speak to you about: 1) why arms control agreements with Russia continue to be an important tool to enhance the security of the United States, our allies and partners; 2) how we have used numerous arms control tools since the crisis in Ukraine began to increase transparency and stability in support of our broader regional efforts; and 3) the seriousness with which the Administration takes compliance with arms control treaties.

First, as has been recognized for over four decades, arms control is a tool that can be used to enhance the security of the United States, our Allies and our partners. It is one of the many diplomatic, military and economic tools that the United States uses to address 21st Century challenges. Many of our Allies and partners are signatories and States-Parties to these same arms control agreements and we have worked closely with them to negotiate and implement these agreements. The Obama Administration has continued the longstanding bipartisan approach to arms control with Russia that had its origins in the days of the Cold War. The administrations of Presidents Ronald Reagan and George H.W. Bush were the architects of many of our most successful and enduring arms control efforts. Let me affirm that the United States is committed to maintaining strategic stability between the United States and Russia and to encouraging mutual steps to foster a more stable, resilient, predictable, and transparent security relationship.

That said, Russia's illegal actions in Ukraine have undermined trust. While diplomacy between the United States and Russia continues, no one can ignore that Russia's actions in Ukraine have violated the very principles upon which cooperation is built. Further, as we consider arms control priorities this year or in any year, we will continue to consult closely with our allies and partners every step of the way. Our security and defense, as well as that of our allies and partners, is non-negotiable. We will only pursue arms control agreements that advance our national interest.

The New START Treaty and Next Steps

During the Cold War, Washington and Moscow found it in our mutual interest to work together to cap and then to begin reducing the number of nuclear weapons to reverse the nuclear arms race and improve mutual security and stability. For the same reasons, we judged that the New START was in the U.S. national security interest, and that is why we continue to implement the New START Treaty with Russia even today. We are now in the fourth year of implementation and, despite the crisis in Ukraine, we and Russia continue to implement the Treaty in a business-like manner.

Since entry into force in 2011, the United States has inspected—with boots on the ground—Russian nuclear weapons facilities 58 times. Moreover, the United States and the Russian Federation have exchanged more than six thousand notifications on one another's nuclear forces since entry into force. These notifications provide predictability by enabling the tracking of strategic offensive arms from location to location, giving advance notice of upcoming ballistic missile test launches, and providing updates of changes in the status of systems covered by the Treaty. For example, a notification is sent every time a heavy bomber is moved out of its home base for more than 24 hours. Additionally, when either party conducts a flight test of an ICBM or SLBM, they are required to notify the other party one day in advance.

The Treaty's verification mechanisms allow us to monitor and inspect Russia's strategic nuclear forces to ensure compliance with the Treaty. For both the United States and Russia, accurate and timely knowledge of each other's nuclear forces helps to prevent the risks of misunderstandings, mistrust, and worst-case analysis and worst-case policymaking. Put another way, the New START Treaty's verification regime is a vital tool in ensuring transparency and predictability between the world's largest nuclear powers.

The 2010 Nuclear Posture Review (NPR) highlighted the importance of aligning U.S. forces to address the 21st century security threats. As a result of further analysis called for by the NPR, the President announced in Berlin last June that, after a comprehensive review of our nuclear forces, we have determined that we can ensure the security of the United States and our allies and partners and maintain a strong and credible strategic deterrent while safely pursuing up to a one-third reduction in deployed strategic warheads from the level established in the New START Treaty. We have sought to negotiate reductions with Russia, but to date Russia has not expressed interest in nuclear reductions below the New START levels. We will also continue to work within NATO to develop ideas for reciprocal measures that we could in the future propose to Russia to build confidence and increase transparency with regard to non-strategic nuclear weapons in Europe. This will lay important groundwork for the future when conditions may be more conducive to progress in this area. Any changes to NATO's nuclear posture must be taken by consensus within the Alliance.

Conventional Arms Control

In the realm of conventional arms control, the United States and our Allies have been using arms control mechanisms in an effort to promote stability in Europe, provide transparency on Russia's provocative actions in and around Ukraine, and assure our allies and partners in the face of Russian aggression.

The Vienna Document on Confidence and Security Building Measures is a series of politically binding confidence and security-building measures (CSBMs) designed to increase openness and transparency concerning military activities conducted inside the OSCE's zone of application (ZOA), which includes the territory, surrounding sea areas, and air space of all European (Russia from the western border to the Ural Mountains) and Central Asian participating States. The Vienna Document allows for a variety of information exchanges, on-site inspections, evaluation visits, observation visits, and other military-to-military contacts to take place according to Vienna Document provisions. In the case of the United States, only military forces and activities inside the ZOA are impacted.

It was designed to increase openness and transparency on military activities across Europe and Russia. Since the crisis in Ukraine began, Allies and partners from six countries have participated in four Vienna Document inspections in Russia and Ukraine. Using additional Vienna Document provisions, inspectors continue a near-continuous presence in Ukraine, providing insight into events there. So far, inspectors from 16 countries have participated in five such missions since March 20.

Ukraine has also implemented provisions of the Vienna Document in order to host observers to dispel any concerns about its own military activities by inviting all OSCE participating States to Ukraine from March 5-20. A total of 77 people from 32 OSCE states and the OSCE Secretariat participated in this visit. Ukraine called on Russia to host a similar visit in western Russia near the border with Ukraine, but Russia has not offered to do so.

The use of these tools in Ukraine demonstrates that the Vienna Document can help provide insight and transparency into military activities during a crisis. However, it is not designed to address a crisis when one OSCE participating State ignores the OSCE principles and commitments it has undertaken. Moving forward, the United States will work with our Allies and partners to develop ideas to update the Vienna Document to reflect lessons learned.

The United States and its Treaty partners have also made active use of the Open Skies Treaty to monitor events in Ukraine and Russia. The Open Skies treaty establishes a regime of aerial observation flights over the territories of its signatories. The Treaty is designed to enhance mutual understanding and confidence by giving Treaty partners the ability to gather information through aerial imaging on military forces and activities of concern to them. During special OSCE meetings on April 7 and 17 that were convened under Vienna Document provisions to address unusual military activities, the U.S. delegation was able to display Open Skies Treaty imagery of the Russian forces, in order to show that concerns about Russia's actions and military movements are valid and disturbing. Unfortunately, the Russian Federation has refused to provide information that could dispel the concerns of other states.

Since the Ukraine crisis began, the United States and 15 Treaty partners have flown 11 missions over Ukraine and Western Russia yielding imagery of thousands of square miles of territory. These flights have resulted in valuable data and insights for not only the United States but our partners and allies who are also States Parties.

One particularly notable event which has occurred in light of the crisis: the Treaty's provision for "Extraordinary Observation Flights" was invoked for the first time. Per Ukraine's request, two extraordinary flights were conducted over Ukrainian territory to observe whether Russia forces had moved beyond Crimea. In response to this request, Sweden flew from Kiev south to Odessa, with observers from Norway, Belgium, and the UK on March 13. On March 14, the U.S. flew along Ukraine's eastern border with Russia, with observers from Canada and Estonia. These flights provided reassurance to Ukraine and demonstrated our commitment to work with Allies to uphold key elements of the Euro-Atlantic security architecture. The following week, Russia accepted an extraordinary flight by Ukraine over its territory near the border. The U.S. is in Kyiv this week flying another extraordinary flight over eastern Ukraine in response to the latest Russian activities.

Since then, a number of Allies have conducted observation flights in Russia. We are working closely with Allies to maximize the benefit of these missions, coordinating on mission planning as well as sharing imagery and analysis. As an example of the utility of these flights, the German/U.S. mission on March 24 over Russia near the border with Ukraine provided unclassified imagery helping substantiate Russian military activity in Belgorod, Boguchar, and Rostov despite Russia's denials.

We believe these arms control mechanisms have great importance not only in providing insight and transparency into Russian actions in and around Ukraine, but demonstrating support for our allies and partners in ensuring their sovereignty and territorial integrity. More broadly, such mechanisms contribute to greater transparency and stability in the Euro-Atlantic region.

I want to underscore that our NATO allies and other partners in Europe are strong supporters of arms control in Europe and our active participation and leadership in those efforts.

Compliance Report

Let me turn now to the issue of compliance. First and foremost, the Administration takes compliance with all arms control agreements extremely seriously. For this reason, this Administration worked hard to produce a compliance report in July of 2010 – the first delivered to Congress after a five year lapse – and has produced one every year since. Prior to this Administration, 2005 was the last year that a report had been delivered to Congress.

We endeavor every year to produce a compliance report by April 15. This is challenging, as the reporting period ends at the end of each calendar year, leaving us just three and one half months to gather the necessary input from the Departments of State, Defense, and Energy, as well as the Intelligence Community. Given the volume of information and seriousness with which the Administration conducts its annual compliance review, a thorough collecting, weighing, and reviewing of all available information throughout the reporting period is required and takes time. As such, despite our best efforts we have not always been able to complete the coordination process in time to provide the report by April 15. This will be true again this year, however, the report will be fully coordinated and available later in the spring. The report is currently in final interagency review.

Let me add that when countries do not uphold their arms control obligations, we hold them accountable. Russia ceased implementation of its Conventional-Armed Forces in Europe Treaty (CFE) obligations in December 2007. After two intense diplomatic efforts to break the impasse and encourage Russia to resume implementation, in November 2011, the United States ceased carrying out certain obligations under the CFE Treaty with regard to Russia. We were joined by our NATO Allies that are party to the Treaty, as well as Georgia and Moldova, in taking this step – in all, 24 of the 30 countries that are party to the Treaty.

As we have previously stated, we have concerns about Russian compliance with the INF Treaty. We have raised them with Russia and are pressing for clear answers in an effort to resolve our concerns because of the importance of the INF Treaty to Euro-Atlantic security. We've briefed our NATO allies on our concerns and will continue to coordinate with them on this and other matters that affect our common security. We have been keeping Congress informed on this matter through briefings with relevant congressional committees and will continue to do so. We will continue to work with Russia to resolve our concerns, and to encourage mutual steps to help foster a more stable, resilient, transparent security relationship. We're not going to drop the issue until our concerns have been addressed. As I hope you understand, I am not able to go more deeply into this subject in an open hearing, and would ask that you not press me to do so in open session.

As another example of how we seek to address compliance concerns, several years ago we had questions with regard to China's implementation of the Chemical Weapons Convention. Through active engagement with Chinese officials about whether China should have declared production and subsequent consumption of a particular chemical, our technical experts outlined U.S. concerns and China addressed each of our questions in a collegial and productive manner to close out this issue.

Conclusion

Arms control treaties and agreements continue to be an important tool that can enhance the security of the United States and our friends and allies. The successful implementation of the New START Treaty, and the important contributions that the Open Skies Treaty and the Vienna Document have played recently in Ukraine, demonstrate the continued relevance of arms control for our national security. Thank you very much. I look forward to your questions.

———

Mr. POE. Thank you, Ms. Friedt.

Mr. Hartley, we just have a few minutes left in the voting process so we will do your testimony as soon as we come back.

We have two votes. After the second vote is concluded we will start immediately after that and we will hear what you have to say. Committee is in recess.

[Recess.]

STATEMENT OF MR. BRENT HARTLEY, DEPUTY ASSISTANT SECRETARY, BUREAU OF EUROPEAN AND EURASIAN AFFAIRS, U.S. DEPARTMENT OF STATE

Mr. HARTLEY. Thank you very much, Mr. Chairman, members of the committees. I appreciate very much your inviting me to testify here today on our efforts to reassure allies and partners and to bolster security in Ukraine and the region, and I would like to thank the members of both subcommittees or both committees for your engagement on European security in light of the Ukraine crisis.

It is important to remember how we got to this point. Russia's illegal annexation and occupation of Crimea and its continued campaign to undermine and intimidate the Government of Ukraine have up-ended the post-Cold War security architecture that Russia had in fact helped to create.

Russia is maintaining a 40,000—a contingent of 40,000 troops on Ukraine's eastern border and conducting military activities that raise deep concerns. There is strong evidence demonstrating that the actions of recent weeks—the roadblocks, building seizures, hostage takings and other violent acts in Eastern Ukraine, primarily in the Donetsk Oblast—have not been a spontaneous set of events but rather a well orchestrated campaign led by Russian special services.

We strongly condemn the abduction last Friday of the German-led Vienna Document inspection team and their Ukrainian escorts in Slovyansk by pro-Russian separatists.

We are deeply disappointed that senior officials in Moscow have not condemned the abduction of the team nor have they demanded the team's immediate release.

Russia's aggressive actions in Ukraine are in violation of international law and do not uphold the letter or the spirit of the April 17th Geneva statement.

Yesterday, the United States acted, imposing new sanctions on seven Russian Government officials including two members of President Putin's inner circle and 17 companies linked to Putin's inner circle.

These steps demonstrate that the United States is committed to increase the costs on Russia as it persists in its efforts to destabilize Ukraine and that we will hold Russia accountable for its provocative actions.

Russia's actions have also forced the United States and NATO allies to fundamentally reexamine our strategic engagement in Europe. My testimony today will focus on three areas of this effort.

First, I will talk about efforts to reassure NATO's front line allies and to bolster our other partners in the region. Second, I will discuss the Organization for Security and Cooperation in Europe's important role in monitoring the security situation and facilitating dialogue in Ukraine. Third, I will address U.S. bilateral security assistance to Ukraine.

First, we are pursuing measures through NATO and bilaterally to reassure our allies and partners in the region and in particular to demonstrate our solemn commitment to our collective defense responsibilities to our NATO allies. We have deployed six additional F–15s to the Baltic air policing mission.

We have deployed 12 F–16s and other aircraft and personnel for exercises—joint U.S.-Polish exercises coordinated by the U.S. aviation training detachment in Lask, Poland.

NATO has deployed AWACS to provide aerial surveillance over Poland and Romania as well as a mine counter measure naval group into the Baltic Sea. The United States deployed—has deployed ships into the Black Sea for exercises with Romania and Bulgaria.

On April 16th, NATO allies agreed on additional measures to provide reassurance and demonstrate NATO's resolve and solidarity. U.S. Army in Europe has deployed over the last week company-sized contingents of paratroopers to Poland, Latvia, Lithuania and Estonia for exercises with those host governments' troops.

These will be the first in a series of expanded land-force training exercises in the region that will take place at least through the end of the year. As we prepare for the NATO summit in Wales, it will be an opportunity to reassess the alliance's long-term priorities in the wake of Russia's aggressive actions in Ukraine—that, along with NATO-Ukraine relations questions related to the open-door NATO enlargement, Afghanistan capabilities and enhancing NATO partnerships.

Beyond NATO's borders, we are engaged with other front line states like Georgia and Moldova and I would be happy to get into more detail on that in my—in the question and answer period.

Second, we see a vital role for the OSCE in this crisis. Along with our allies in Europe we are committed to maintaining a large presence of international monitors as part of the OSCE special monitoring mission.

This mission is positioned to objectively assess the security situation and investigate claims of human rights abuses as well as to assist in de-escalating tensions in Eastern Ukraine.

But for this mission to be properly implemented in accordance with the Geneva statement, Russia must take active and concrete steps immediately to de-escalate the crisis including public and private messages to pro-Russian elements engaged in illegal activities in Ukraine as well as active support for the monitoring missions role.

OSCE is also involved in election observation for the May 25th election. The Office for Democratic Institutions and Human Rights, or ODIHR, is laying the groundwork for the largest observation mission in its history—in its 40-year history, planning to deploy approximately 1,000 observers in the run-up to the election.

Third, we are working with the Ukrainian Government to provide security assistance. As Vice President Biden announced last week, we are providing $8 million in assistance to allow the Ukrainian armed forces and border guard service to fulfill core security missions.

This is in addition to the $3 million of meals ready to eat, $3.5 million of health and welfare assistance to the armed forces and $3 million in other security assistance to Ukraine's state border guard service.

Looking forward, the United States will continue to reaffirm the security and stability of the region across multiple fronts using multiple tools at our disposal.

In this effort, we appreciate Congress' bipartisan attention and support for Ukraine and for stability across the region and will continue to work in close coordination with you on all three of these areas.

Chair, thank you very much and I look forward to your questions.

[The prepared statement of Mr. Hartley follows:]

Brent Hartley
Deputy Assistant Secretary of State for European and Eurasian Affairs
April 29, 2014
Written Testimony

Thank you for inviting me to testify here today on our efforts to reassure Allies and partners and bolster security in Ukraine and the region.

I would like to start by expressing my gratitude to the members at this joint subcommittee hearing for your engagement on European security in light of events in Ukraine. The travel of Judge Poe and other members of this committee to Kyiv and Dnipropetrovsk last week sent a strong signal that the United States stands with the Ukrainian people at this critical moment.

Before I begin, it is important to remember how we got here. Russia's illegal annexation and occupation of Crimea and its continued campaign to undermine and intimidate the government of Ukraine have upended the post-Cold War security architecture that Russia helped to create. Russia is maintaining a 40,000 troop contingent on Ukraine's Eastern border and conducting military activities that raise concerns. The Russian government is attempting to delegitimize the interim Ukrainian government through a sustained propaganda and disinformation campaign. There is strong evidence demonstrating that the actions of recent weeks – the road blocks, building seizures, hostage-taking and other violent acts – primarily in Donetsk oblast – have not been a spontaneous set of events, but rather a well-orchestrated campaign led by Russian special services. We strongly condemn the abduction last Friday of a German-led Vienna Document inspection team and their Ukrainian escorts in Slovyansk by pro-Russian separatists. We are disappointed that senior officials in Moscow have not condemned the abduction of the team and demanded the team's immediate release.

Russia's aggressive actions in Ukraine are in violation of international law and do not uphold the letter or the spirit of the April 17th Geneva Accord. The G7 issued a joint statement over the weekend stating that we will "swiftly impose further sanctions on Russia over the Ukraine crisis" citing Russia's continued provocative actions that "escalate tensions by increasingly concerning rhetoric and ongoing threatening military maneuvers on Ukraine's border."

And yesterday the United States acted – imposing new sanctions on seven Russian government officials, including two members of President Putin's inner circle and 17 companies linked to Putin's inner circle. In addition, the Department of Commerce has added additional restrictions on 13 of those companies by imposing a license requirement with a presumption of denial for the export, re-export or other foreign transfer of U.S.-origin items to the companies. Further, today the Departments of Commerce and State have announced a tightened policy to deny export license applications for any high-technology items that could contribute to Russia's military capabilities. These steps demonstrate that the United States is committed to increase costs on

Russia if it persists in its efforts to destabilize Ukraine and will hold Russia accountable for its provocative actions.

Russia's actions have also forced the United States and NATO Allies to fundamentally reexamine our strategic engagement in Europe. The United States remains as committed as ever to the stability of the region. And we are working through all available bilateral and multilateral channels to ensure that security and stability in the region are maintained. My testimony today will focus on three areas of this effort. First, I will talk about effort to reassure NATO's frontline Allies and bolster our other partners in the region. Second, I will discuss the Organization for Security and Cooperation in Europe's (OSCE) important role in monitoring the security situation and facilitating dialogue in Ukraine. Third, I will address U.S. bilateral security assistance to Ukraine.

Reassuring NATO Allies and Partners on the Frontlines

First, we are pursuing measures, through NATO and bi-laterally, to reassure our Allies and partners in the region and in particular to demonstrate our solemn commitment to our collective defense responsibilities to our NATO Allies. As President Obama said before his meeting with Secretary General Rasmussen in Brussels last month: "We have to have the resources and the preparation to make sure that every member of NATO feels confident in Article 5's effect." Following Russia's illegal annexation and occupation of the Crimea region of Ukraine, the United States and its Allies in NATO undertook immediate steps to provide visible reassurance to Allies in Central and Eastern Europe.

We deployed 6 additional F-15s to the Baltic Air Policing mission. We added 12 additional F-16s, three C-130s and 200 additional U.S. personnel to the U.S.-Poland Aviation Training Detachment in Lask, Poland. NATO deployed AWACS to provide aerial surveillance over Poland and Romania. The United States deployed the USS TRUXTUN and later the USS DONALD COOK to the Black Sea for exercises. The USS TAYLOR is there now.

On April 16, NATO Allies agreed on additional measures to provide reassurance and demonstrate NATO's resolve and solidarity. As Secretary General Rasmussen said, this will mean "more planes in the air, more ships on the water, and more readiness on land."

The tangible impact of this decision can already be seen on the ground in Europe. The U.S. Army Europe is deploying forces to NATO frontline states at their request to conduct expanded U.S. land force training. On April 23rd, a company-sized contingent of U.S. paratroopers arrived in Poland to begin exercises with Polish troops. This exercise will be the first in a series of expanded U.S. Army land force training activities in the region that will take place at least through the end of this year. Additional companies have moved to Lithuania, Latvia and Estonia for similar exercises. These events are in addition to previously scheduled multinational land force military exercises in the region aimed at assuring regional allies of the U.S. unwavering commitment to NATO.

We are committed, along with NATO Allies, to maintain a persistent rotational presence in frontline NATO states to reassure our Allies and prepare for any contingency to meet our Article 5 obligations. The United States is doing its part and Allies are stepping up as well. Now more than ever it is incumbent upon all NATO members to contribute actively and equitably to the assets of the Alliance.

The United States is preparing for the NATO Summit in Wales in September. It will be an opportunity to reassess the alliance's long term priorities in the wake of Russia's aggressive actions in Ukraine, ensure an enhanced presence along NATO members' borders through the employment of land, sea and air capabilities and reaffirm NATO's Open Door policy under Article 10 of the Washington Treaty remains a bedrock principle of the Alliance.

As part of this work, we will renew our efforts to encourage Allies to reverse the downward trend in their defense spending to make them more capable of contributing to the growing needs of the Alliance. Both the President during his March visit to Brussels and Secretary Kerry at the April 1-2 NATO Foreign Ministerial meeting underscored the need for Allies to step up their defense spending, especially on priority capabilities, and this issue will continue to be a key priority in the run-up to the NATO summit in Wales.

Beyond NATO's borders, we are engaged with other frontline states like Georgia and Moldova who have also come under pressure as a result of Russia's illegal use of force in the region. The United States continues to support Georgia's efforts to build a consensus within NATO for offering Georgia a Membership Action Plan. And Assistant Secretary Nuland and senior DoD officials traveled to Moldova in recent weeks. Both states plan to sign Association Agreements with the EU by June. We welcome both countries' progress toward deeper European integration and are in consultation with both to intensify our political and economic assistance.

Working with OSCE in the Pursuit of Comprehensive Security in Ukraine

Second, we see a vital role for the OSCE in this crisis. The United States remains committed to de-escalation and a diplomatic off-ramp if Russia chooses to take it. We stand behind the Joint Geneva statement that the OSCE should play a "leading role in assisting Ukrainian authorities and local communities in the immediate implementation of these de-escalation measures wherever they are needed most."

Along with our allies in Europe, we are committed to maintaining a large presence of international monitors as part of the OSCE's Special Monitoring Mission. This mission is positioned to objectively assess the security situation and investigate claims of human rights abuses and to play a leading role in assisting Ukrainian authorities and local communities in the immediate implementation of de-escalation measures. As of April 25, the Special Monitoring Mission had 161 staff in country, including about 121 monitors in the field from 45 countries. We commend their work and support the OSCE moving ahead quickly to increase the number of monitors up to 500. The Special Monitoring Mission is providing public reports on the security situation and reported incidents concerning violations of human rights and OSCE commitments. The Mission's mandate also serves to facilitate dialogue in order to reduce tensions and promote peace and stability.

In Geneva, the United States, Ukraine, Russia and the EU discussed how the Special Monitoring Mission could do more to assist with the return of government buildings held by armed pro-Russia separatists in eastern Ukraine. The United States supports the Special Monitoring Mission's efforts to foster resolution as illegal armed separatist groups disarm, seized buildings are returned, and illegally occupied places are vacated. But for those commitments to be properly implemented, Russia must take active and concrete steps immediately to de-escalate the crisis, including public and private messages to pro-Russian elements engaged in illegal activities in Ukraine as well as active support for the OSCE Monitoring Mission's role.

In addition, the OSCE's Office for Democratic Institutions and Human Rights (ODIHR) is laying the groundwork to assess the country's electoral process for compliance with international standards for democratic elections. All told, ODIHR is preparing to deploy approximately 1,000 observers throughout the country to monitor the May 25 elections in one of the largest monitoring missions in the 40 year history of the organization. For election day observation, ODIHR will join efforts with a delegation of the OSCE Parliamentary Assembly, including a delegation of the Congressional Helsinki Commission led by Senator Cardin, and other parliamentary partners.

As the Vice President said last week in Kyiv, "This may be the most important election in the history of Ukraine. This is a chance to make good on the aspirations of the overwhelming majority of Ukrainians east and west and every part of this country." The United States is proud to support and actively participate in the OSCE's election observation mission and we will provide approximately fifteen percent of the short- and long-term observers. On April 17, ODIHR released its first interim observation report on Ukraine's Early Presidential Elections. The report notes that progress towards the administration of elections has been largely positive, although the ongoing political and security developments may pose challenges, particularly in the east.

The OSCE experts – those in the special monitoring mission and those serving as election observers – are the international community's eyes and ears on the ground in Ukraine. We rely on their presence, their mediation efforts, and their reports to portray an accurate picture of the events in Ukraine and defray any attempt by the Russian government to undermine the electoral process or further destabilize Ukraine. These monitors must be allowed to do their jobs without interference, provocation or violence directed against them.

Providing non-lethal security assistance to Ukraine

Third, we are working with the Ukrainian Ministry of Defense to provide security assistance at this critical time.

As Vice President Biden announced last week, we are providing $8 million in assistance to allow the Ukrainian armed forces and Border Guard Service to fulfill their core security missions. This is in addition to the $3 million of Meals Ready to Eat (MREs), $3.5 million of health and welfare assistance to the armed forces, and $3 million in other security assistance to Ukraine's State Border Guard Service that the United States is already providing to Ukraine. We have also carried out two extraordinary Open Skies observation missions over Ukraine at the request of the Ukrainian government and are participating in ongoing military observation missions under the Vienna Document.

These are first steps, not the limits of our assistance. Going forward, U.S. and Ukrainian officials will remain in constant consultation on how the United States can best enhance bilateral cooperation with the Ukrainian defense establishment. The outlines of our security assistance engagement will come into clearer focus following consultation and approval by the new government after the May 25th elections. We are reviewing other means of assisting Ukraine to pursue modernization, defense reform and border security.

Conclusion

During his visit to Kyiv last week, Vice President Biden expressed our solidarity with Ukraine when he told Prime Minister Yatsenyuk that "You will not walk this road alone. We will walk with you." But the scope of this commitment goes far beyond Ukraine.

Our commitment to NATO's Article 5 guarantee remains—as it has always been— ironclad. And our adherence to OSCE principles and commitments as a means to provide comprehensive security remains steadfast.

Looking forward, the United States will continue to reaffirm the security and stability of the region across multiple fronts using multiple tools at our disposal. In this effort, we appreciate Congress's bipartisan attention and support for security assistance in Ukraine and across the region and will continue work in close coordination with you on all three of these areas.

Thank you and I look forward to your questions.

Mr. POE. Thanks for yielding back time. The Chair will now recognize the chairman of the Subcommittee on Europe, Eurasia, and Emerging Threats—Mr. Rohrabacher—for 5 minutes of questions.

Mr. ROHRABACHER. Thank you very much, Mr. Chairman. The focus of this hearing, we originally thought would be our nuclear weapons and the relationship between the United States and Russia in terms of cooperating on reducing and restricting the number of nuclear weapons that threaten human kind.

We have gone beyond that and we, of course—however, I believe the purpose of that is to put in perspective the decisions we must make in terms of weapons control after the events that have happened in Ukraine.

Let me just note that from my perspective, there has been too gleeful a response by so many of my former colleagues, and I am not talking about members of the House. I am talking about people who have worked with me over the years in various administrations and various anti-Communist causes.

There seems to be a gleeful response to what has happened in Ukraine because it then gives them yet a purpose in going back and beating up the old enemy. And, frankly, the Soviet Union was our enemy because it was directed by people with an ideology that it was trying to supplant in the rest of the world and doing so in a big way as well as building up their own military. Russia is a powerful force in the world, which we need to deal with as a major country—a major nation.

Major countries have their interests. I do not see what is going on in Ukraine as a—as a outcome of the Communist ideology but instead you have a very important international power there, Russia, that is governed by someone who is looking out for its national interests and who that leadership of that country, obviously, believes that what was going on in Ukraine was contrary to their national interests and that they were not being treated fairly in a way in which a pro-Russian leader was removed from office by street violence rather than by elections, which was going to result in their losing the—what they had was access to the Crimea and a port for their fleet.

That said, I would like to go back to the original purpose that we came here today was to talk about arms control and how that will be impacted by this new shift in our relations with Russia, and I say that no matter what I just said the bottom line is it is in recognition that we are now not in as a positive relationship or a neutral relationship that we were in 2 years ago with Russia.

We are in fact in a—things have—our relationship with Russia has deteriorated. Whose fault that is and does the Russian Government—does Putin and—we share—have all the blame or do we share some of it or was there a power grab by the EU? That is something that would take long to discuss. But the fact is we know that relationship has deteriorated.

What I would like to ask the panel is does this mean that what we negotiated with—and I am very proud of what Ronald Reagan accomplished in eliminating a whole classification of nuclear weapons and brought down the number of nuclear weapons that threaten the world—does that mean that we can no longer work with Russia in this area?

Should we postpone our efforts or pull back from cooperation with the current Russian Government on those issues? Should we then also pull back from economic cooperation?

Should we declare the space program that we are in partners with Russia now to be not something that we believe we can count on and thus we should go the opposite direction? What about that?

What are the implications for arms control? What are the implications for cooperating in other areas with Russia on this whole Ukrainian situation?

Ms. FRIEDT. Thank you, Mr. Chairman. I will be pleased to answer that question.

First of all, I would say that this administration has made it very clear that it is important to continue to cooperate with Russia where we can, where our national security interests coincide. But then when we disagree we disagree and we make our disagreement very clear.

So there is no question that it is in our national security interest to continue to work with Russia and international partners in multilateral efforts that are key to global security.

Such efforts as elimination of Syria chemical weapons, for example, our work together on Iran and, I would add, also our work together in the arms control field, and that means a continued implementation of arms control——

Mr. ROHRABACHER. So we are not advocating—so the administration and what you are suggesting today—good policy would be not to punish Russia in those areas for what they are doing in Ukraine?

Ms. FRIEDT. I would not say punish. We have a very clear position on the events in Ukraine and——

Mr. ROHRABACHER. So we should not let cooperation be a tool then. Mr. Hartley, could you answer that and then I will—I have already taken too much time. I am sorry.

Mr. HARTLEY. Yes, sir. Thank you for that question. Well, as Anita said we—there are areas where both we and the Russians perceive our national interest to coincide and Anita outlined a number of them. One area where we now have a very profound difference is over what the post-Cold War European security environment should be—what the ground rules are.

Coming out of the Cold War, we had—we thought some very clear rules based on the Helsinki Final Act of 1975 and other agreements that European borders would not be changed by force.

The Russians have undertaken to do that with regard to Crimea. We believe that they are actively involved using their special forces and other agents to destabilize Eastern Ukraine and it is for that reason because of this behavior contrary——

Mr. ROHRABACHER. Thank you. Thank you very much. And Mr. Chairman, again, as we discuss this China is still in the world and in the picture and I hope that as we look and we work these problems out that we keep in mind that China has to be part of the equation or the world will be less secure.

Thank you very much, Mr. Chairman.

Mr. POE. I thank the gentleman. I will—the Chair will recognize the ranking member of the subcommittee from California, Mr. Sherman, for 5 minutes.

Mr. SHERMAN. This has become to some extent a Ukraine hearing and we are honored by the presence of the deputy assistant secretary from the relevant bureau.

Mr. Hartley, has the Ukrainian Government been successful in disarming anti-Russia militias?

Mr. HARTLEY. Thank you, sir, for that question. My expertise falls more on the NATO, the OSCE and the bilateral security assistance side. It is my impression that they have made some progress there but I would be happy to take that question for a more authoritative response.

Mr. SHERMAN. Okay. While you take that question, the other question is what are we doing to urge the government in Kiev to honor and even make less subject to alteration statutes adopted in the past to assure the Russian language would be an official language in the south and east of Ukraine?

What are we doing to say yes, there may be forces—political forces in Kiev that say let us impose the Ukrainian language on everyone and there may be forces on the other side?

I for one understand America is spending its treasure and taking risks for the territorial integrity of the Ukraine. I am an agnostic as to what language should be spoken in the East and I would hate to think that we find ourselves exposed to risk and cost because the noncompromising elements prevail in Kiev on these language issues.

Ms. Friedt, what—does Russia put forward any arguments that we are in violation of any of the arms control agreements that we have entered into with Russia or with its predecessor government?

Ms. FRIEDT. Thank you for that question, sir. Yes, as a matter of fact Russia, when we issue our annual compliance report every year, at least this administration, the Russians regularly come back with some—their own——

Mr. SHERMAN. So they have an annual compliance report which may even be issued on time. Sorry about that. Sorry. Go ahead. And what do you think is their strongest complaint?

Ms. FRIEDT. Strongest complaint, the one I would say—I can't give you all of their complaints right now because I haven't looked at them recently but certainly our missile defense is what they focus on.

Mr. SHERMAN. And which treaty do they believe the missile defense efforts are in violation of?

Ms. FRIEDT. Well, it would be more than likely the INF treaty is one.

Mr. SHERMAN. Okay. Now, as—I am trying to understand what is the legal obligation of Russia with regard to intermediate missiles that they claim will be used only in naval warfare.

As I understand it, they are allowed to test these missiles from a ground-based launcher but not if that ground-based launcher would be the effective launcher to use in case hostilities broke out. What are they allowed to do on land in order to test weapons that they say are exclusively for naval use?

Ms. FRIEDT. Sir, quite frankly, thank you for your question. I am not prepared right now to go into technical details. The focus here is——

Mr. SHERMAN. I am asking you what the treaty provides. I am asking for you to just inform us what the treaty provides. What is the United States allowed to do? What is the—and I am not asking for a secret here.

Ms. FRIEDT. No, no. Not at all a secret. But let me just briefly state that what, as I mentioned before, that we have very serious concerns and as you have stated that Russia is developing a ground-launched cruise missile that is inconsistent with the INF treaty and we have made those concerns very clear to the Russians.

Mr. SHERMAN. I am hoping you would make them clear to us. Is the mere testing of—and Mr. Hartley, I don't know if you have a comment on this—the mere testing of this missile a violation if they can claim that it is—that they only plan to deploy it on ships?

Ms. FRIEDT. Sir, that would go into the specific range and such that it is tested. So it——

Mr. SHERMAN. It is being tested for—you know, it is an intermediate range missile. The question is is it a naval intermediate range missile or are they creating a ground-based intermediate missile?

Ms. FRIEDT. Sir, I can't get into details here, I am afraid, on that topic because of the—I would be happy to talk about it in closed——

Mr. SHERMAN. Okay. The details I want are what are the provisions of the treaty but my time has more than expired. I thank you for your time.

Mr. POE. I thank the gentleman. Ms. Friedt, it has taken 5 years for the State Department to reach a verdict on this treaty, in my opinion.

So my question is are the Russians, in our point of view, in violation of the treaty? And I see only one of three answers—yes, no, you don't know. So which one of those is the answer?

Ms. FRIEDT. Sir, we are in the process of finalizing the annual compliance report and we will have a finding so shortly.

Mr. POE. So you can't tell me whether you—it is yes or no or you don't know?

Ms. FRIEDT. I can't at this point because, as I mentioned, it is——

Mr. POE. When are you going to have this report ready? It is—like the ranking member said, it is overdue.

Ms. FRIEDT. Sir——

Mr. POE. It is 5 years taken to get a report here. Either they are in compliance or they are not in compliance. We've got to make foreign policy decisions and we don't know if the Russians are cheating or not? So how long is it going—when are we going to get a verdict on the report?

Ms. FRIEDT. Sir, we report on this issue every year on the INF treaty and at this point the annual compliance report is in the process of being finalized.

Mr. POE. So when will it be finalized?

Ms. FRIEDT. Later this spring.

Mr. POE. You don't know. Okay. Each of you have said that the actions by Putin are illegal. You have seen that there is some dis-

29

agreement here as to whether Russia can do what they are doing internationally or not.

Why is the action of Russia going into Crimea and then now Eastern Europe—Ukraine—illegal in the United States' point of view? You both said it was illegal. So why is it illegal?

Mr. HARTLEY. Yes, sir. Thank you for that question. The—undertaking the actions they did the Russians have violated their commitments under the U.N. charter. That is from a legal standpoint.

From a political standpoint, they have violated—well, they have broken commitments made under the 1994 Budapest memorandum and as well as the commitments under the Helsinki Final Act, among others.

Mr. POE. Ms. Friedt, do you have any other comments other than what Mr. Hartley has already said on why the action is illegal?

Ms. FRIEDT. No, sir. I think Mr. Hartley has answered the question.

Mr. POE. When I was in Ukraine and in recent weeks have talked to other heads of state in the area they are not the only country that is concerned about their territorial integrity—Moldova, other former Soviet republics not yet in NATO and some that are in NATO. Are there concerns warranted? Mr. Hartley.

Mr. HARTLEY. Yes, sir, if I may. The—of course, they——

Mr. POE. And I am talking about concerns of Russia coming in and taking over some of their territory. That is my question.

Mr. HARTLEY. Yes, sir. The actions that the Russians have undertaken with regard to Crimea and what they are doing in Eastern Ukraine gives deep cause for concern on the part of those nations.

Any country that has a Russian minority or a Russian-speaking minority, at least according to Mr. Putin in his March—April 18th speech, according to Mr. Putin's public statements is—would seem at risk of being—be at risk of Russian intervention.

Mr. POE. The Ukrainian Government, on the issue of interest of Russians in the east, there is no definition as to what a Russian is.

Is it a Russian that was born in Russia? Is it a Russian that has moved to Eastern Ukraine? Is it a Russian who wants to be Russian? There is no definition as to what a Russian is.

Do we have a definition of what a Russian is in the eastern part of the Ukraine?

Mr. HARTLEY. I don't know that we do, sir.

Mr. POE. It means different things to different people?

Mr. HARTLEY. That is true, and the way Mr. Putin seems to define it is an ethnic Russian or a Russian speaker.

Mr. POE. The elections in Ukraine are coming up May 26th, I believe. I think it is important for stability in Ukraine that they have these elections, that they are fair, that people vote.

Do you see—I am asking you just to kind of look 26 days in the future—do you see that the Russians may cause a disturbance, a crisis, to try to postpone these elections? It seems like to me they cause a crisis, then they want to solve the crisis by moving in their troops. So are we expecting a possible crisis to try to get these elections postponed?

Mr. HARTLEY. Sir, thank you for that. Well, I would be hesitant to speculate too far into the future. The conditions are such that that is a legitimate concern.

In the negotiation of the Geneva statement, the U.S, the EU and the Ukrainians all urged the inclusion of a sentence that referred to the May 25th elections and the need that they be carried out in an orderly and transparent way.

The Russians refuse to include that in the text of the statement. The disruptions are already taking place in Eastern Ukraine that are bound to complicate the election efforts and we believe that those—that the instability there is being fomented by the Russians.

Mr. POE. Thank you, Mr. Hartley, Ms. Friedt. We will—chair will yield to the gentleman from New York, Mr. Meeks, for 5 minutes.

Mr. MEEKS. Thank you, Mr. Chairman. Let me—you know, there was a beginning where we thought that we would be entering a new world where we would be able to have as we did with the New START treaty, for example, we are not abolishing nuclear weapons altogether. There was a—we were moving in the right direction.

Senate ratified it—the treaty, and the Russian Federation then right after ratified the treaty, and there was a lot of things going on because it seems to me when we are dealing with Crimea and dealing with the east Ukraine we have got to balance a number of issues also—our NATO allies.

I believe that sanctions work but only when they are multilateral sanctions. If we do sanctions individually they are not as strong as they would be multilaterally.

Yet a number of our NATO allies have concerns and we have got to make sure that they are part of whatever we do. We can't separate ourselves, in my viewpoint, from them and that is why our NATO allies are tremendously important.

Some of them are more dependent upon Russia than others and some arms experts—control experts continue to report that Russia could potentially withdraw from treaties such as the INF and that they may further—any further expansion of arms control efforts will likely make no headway for the foreseeable future.

So and some of my colleagues, and I hear some of the pundits, et cetera, saying give weapons and some saying more sanctions. Very few people are talking about diplomatic solutions.

So my first question is do—either one of you do you still see— you know, I always try to believe that there is hope, that we all— we should talk and have conversations with nations that we don't disagree with.

Is diplomacy an option here? Do you see diplomacy having a chance here or have we—you know, or it has no chance? What role do you think diplomacy has in this?

Mr. HARTLEY. Thank you, sir. We believe that diplomacy is a critical aspect of this. That is why Secretary Kerry has had, I forget, six, eight, 10 conversations with Mr. Lavrov, the Russian foreign minister, over the last couple of weeks.

That is why he went to Geneva to negotiate the terms of the Geneva statement that laid out a pathway for de-escalation and so we very much believe that the—that that is the—that diplomacy is the way to resolve this to find a political solution.

The sanctions that we are imposing have been imposed only after those efforts have so far proven fruitless. But our sanctions are scalable. They are flexible. If the Russians make the decision that they want to de-escalate the situation and return to behavior consistent with international norms then we can reverse the sanctions.

But we—even as we go forward, taking a harder line on those, we want to keep the door open for a diplomatic solution.

Mr. MEEKS. And that being the case try to prevent a scenario that we currently have and I do see some of the other regions, whether it is in the Caucuses, the Baltic or the Eastern Europe or Central Asia, you know, we have got to focus on some of those countries now.

I have got a lot of friends in those countries that think Mr. Chairman Poe may have said something. What do we say to them now? What should we do.

I mean, when you look at Ukraine its economy was in the tank and some say Crimea is going to be a big burden on Russia, as it seems right now. But we have got to firm up the rest of the Ukraine economically.

What do you see that we can do? Mr. Hartley, you talked about that there is huge concerns right now about Russia, you know, at least some of these countries about Russia coming in. What can we do now before there is any possibility of Russia invading?

What can we do to help those countries now so that we can make them—assure them that we are there, that NATO is there? What do think we can do right now, prospective?

Mr. HARTLEY. Thank you, sir. Well, with regard to NATO allies, particular those on—we have now come to call front line states, the three Baltic countries—Poland, Romania, Bulgaria—we have already deployed U.S. forces—land, sea and air—and NATO allies are deploying at this point, principally sea and air assets in a measured way to underscore that the Article 5 commitment to collective defense is credible and has teeth. So we are in constant consultation with our NATO allies at NATO headquarters.

Mr. MEEKS. Let me just ask—and we are out of time—I just want to ask this one last question. Do you think Russia is backing down from its arms agreements with the United States and preparing to have a continued military escalation?

You know, that is what some are saying—that in other words, people are saying that Russia is building up and they are strong and kind of daring the United States to have a military escalation on NATO to come up and make them militarily see that that is part and parcel of what is going on here?

Ms. FRIEDT. Sir, thank you for that question. That is precisely why the New START treaty is so important. The fact that we have—and the fact that it has been successfully implemented since it was signed and inspections began in 2011.

Russians are implementing the New START treaty and it does set the limits on their ability to build up nuclear forces.

Mr. MEEKS. And you don't see them violating that right now?

Ms. FRIEDT. No, sir. No, sir.

Mr. MEEKS. Okay. So there is still cooperation in that regards.

Ms. FRIEDT. Yes, sir.

Mr. MEEKS. And there are a number of other things that they are still cooperating with us on?

Ms. FRIEDT. Yes, sir.

Mr. MEEKS. Thank you, Mr. Chairman. I yield back.

Mr. POE. The gentleman yields back.

Mr. HARTLEY. May I add to that, sir, or do you want to move on?

Mr. POE. If you can make it brief.

Mr. HARTLEY. Okay. On the conventional side, the Russians have been modernizing but—and it has been a source of some concern. But we feel as though the assets available to the NATO alliance are sufficient to deter any incursions on NATO territory.

Mr. POE. Thank you, Mr. Hartley. The Chair will recognize the gentleman from Pennsylvania, Mr. Perry.

Mr. PERRY. Thanks, Mr. Chairman. Ladies and gentlemen, appreciate your time. Ms. Friedt, the State Department is aware that Russia may have been in violation of the 1987 Intermediate Range Nuclear Forces Treaty while negotiating the New START treaty.

The first question is when, as far as you understand it, did the administration first learn of the possible violation of the INF treaty by the Russians? Was it in 2008?

Ms. FRIEDT. Sir, the New START treaty—ratification of the New START treaty did not—I mean, at that time the—Russia was implementing the INF treaty successfully. At this point, I would go into—prefer to go into closed sessions to deal with the circumstances, the specific dates on the specific questions you asked.

Mr. PERRY. Okay. Then let me ask you this. When the President was overheard talking to Medvedev at the time he said that after the election he could be more flexible, and this is in the context of Members of Congress being concerned about our national security posture and our ability to secure our nation in light of adversaries and enemies, if you want to call some folks that. What did he mean by that? What do you think he meant by that?

Ms. FRIEDT. Sir, what I can say here is that the United States and this administration will only pursue arms control agreements that are in the United States national security interest and that is something that this administration and the President believes.

Mr. PERRY. But if we know or if we suspect with some credibility that our partner in negotiation is cheating at the time we are negotiating a reduction in our capability, how is that—and we don't take that into account and we continue to march forward with our reduction, how—can you explain to me how that is in our best interest?

Ms. FRIEDT. Sir, as I mentioned in my statement, this administration takes compliance with arms control treaties very seriously. During the negotiation of the New START treaty, we took compliance with arms control treaties into consideration.

Mr. PERRY. But we knew or we suspected? We suspected while we were negotiating the treaty that they were cheating and we continued forward, and it is fine to continue forward with the negotiation. We, as far as you know, and as far as Russia is concerned, based on your testimony have upheld our end of the bargain.

We still don't know—according to your testimony, we won't know until later this spring, and by the way, spring is almost over—to the extent of their cheating and I recognize and acknowledge the sensitivity of the date.

So I will be happy to talk to you in closed session about that. But my concern is that we are unilaterally disarming America while we know or we suspect with some certainty that Russia is cheating on their end of the deal and I still don't understand how that is in our best interest.

Ms. FRIEDT. Thank you for that question, sir. The United States—arms control is in the United States' national security interest.

Mr. PERRY. It is in our interest when we are controlling theirs or they are controlling theirs within the paradigm as well as ours. But it is not in our interest when we are controlling ours and they are not controlling theirs to our satisfaction in accordance with the previous agreement. Would you agree?

Ms. FRIEDT. Sir, we take compliance—this administration takes compliance with arms control very seriously. I am happy to discuss the specifics in closed session.

Let me say with respect to the START treaty that was a very carefully negotiated agreement based on the nuclear posture review. That was a document that received interagency—a very close study by then Secretary Gates and by then chairman of the——

Mr. PERRY. But does it—but did they have the knowledge at that time? Because we didn't—and again, maybe you want to wait to a closed session but it is my understanding that we didn't report our suspicion or our knowledge of their breach of the previous treaty while the negotiation was happening to our NATO allies.

Did our negotiators—did Secretary Gates—did he know at that time while he was in agreement with this accord that we had a very strong suspicion that they were cheating on the previous agreement?

Ms. FRIEDT. Sir, I would like to take you up on your offer to do this in closed session.

Mr. PERRY. All right. Then moving on, based on—based on recent actions in Crimea, can—how do you—do you think the American people should trust the Russians to adhere to a bilateral and multilateral arms control agreement, and if so, why?

Ms. FRIEDT. Sir, this administration believes in trust but verify. So verification and compliance with arms control treaties is very important.

Mr. PERRY. Let me ask you one final question, with due indulgence, Mr. Chairman.

So if we find out and if we prove and in the spring time if it is determined and you report that they had indeed cheated, for lack of a better phrase, on the previous treaty, the previous agreement, what will be the ramifications?

Ms. FRIEDT. Sir, I am not prepared to discuss this at this point. When the report is finalized we will discuss it.

Mr. PERRY. Thank you, Mr. Chairman. I yield.

Mr. POE. Gentleman yields back his time. The Chair will recognize the gentleman from Florida, Mr. Yoho, for 5 minutes.

Mr. YOHO. Thank you, Mr. Chairman, and I appreciate it—your testimony today.

Why do you think Russia has become so emboldened here, going back to August 2010, as far as invading other countries? I thought it was a simple question. I am sorry.

Mr. HARTLEY. Thank you, sir. If only there were simple questions in this life. The—it is, of course, difficult to know precisely why the Russians and Mr. Putin have taken the actions they have.

There are factors related to history, factors related to concern about the influence that a successful democracy and market economy on its border by a land—a country that used to be part of Russia might have on the—or part of the Russian empire might have on the rest of the population in Russia.

Mr. YOHO. Okay. Let me—let me go in a different direction here. As you said, there are the simple questions but the answers aren't often simple. Do you see the 2010 START treaty with us reducing our weapons to 1,550 and with President Obama and the administration willingness to reduce further unilateral cuts to 1,000 do you think that has emboldened the Russians—Mr. Putin and the Russians?

Ms. FRIEDT. Thank you for that question, sir. No, I do not.

Mr. YOHO. Okay. Do you see Russia viewing us as weak, undecisive, not willing? Our credibility has been damaged. If you go back over the course of the last 2 or 3 years—you know, red lines, no red lines, regimes must change, we never said regimes must change, not fulfilling the missile defense system in Poland and, you know, putting a stop to that? Do you think they see us as just kind being weak and not with strong resolve?

Ms. FRIEDT. Sir, I do not see U.S. foreign policy as weak.

Mr. YOHO. Okay. How about you, Mr. Hartley?

Mr. HARTLEY. No, sir. I agree with Anita.

Mr. YOHO. All right. So with what is going on in Venezuela in our own back yard, with what China is doing drawing an arbitrary no-fly zone with Syria and Iran and Iran is closer to a nuclear weapon—in fact, the last—just here a couple of months ago we were told that Iran would have enough material to develop five to six nuclear bombs within 4 to 5 months, I see—what I am seeing from where I am sitting and what I read is the lone superpower that Bill Clinton talked about that America could no longer afford to be becoming weaker, everybody else is becoming emboldened and I see people flexing their muscles because of our weakness and that lack of resolve that we have.

Where do you think this will lead? Where do you think Russia will end up? Are they going to go into Transnistria? Do you see them going into there? Because that is a large Russian-speaking population. Do either one of you see that?

Mr. HARTLEY. Sir, we see that there is a risk and the Russians have influence in Transnistria. But it is our policy to exact a cost from the Russians for their behavior that is in violation of international norms.

Mr. YOHO. All right. And do you feel the sanctions that we are talking about that we have done do you think they will have any compact on Russia's aggression?

Mr. HARTLEY. Sir, the purpose of the sanctions is to try to influence Russian behavior, to bring it back within international norms.

Mr. YOHO. How is it working so far, Ms. Friedt?

Ms. FRIEDT. Actually, that's Mr.—Brent, go ahead.

Mr. HARTLEY. If I may, sir.

Mr. YOHO. Yes.

Mr. HARTLEY. This could be a long process, sir.

Mr. YOHO. All right. But, again, do we have compliance with other nations? Are they putting strong sanctions in place too or is it just us doing this unilaterally?

Mr. HARTLEY. Sir, yesterday as we announced our third round of sanctions we were joined by the G–7, which includes Japan, Canada and four of the major EU members. But the entire EU also joined.

You could—we could—the Norwegians, who are not part of the EU, also adhere to EU sanctions. So we have a broad international coalition that is focused on bringing Russia back into compliance with international norms.

Mr. YOHO. Let me ask you one other question. Do we have troops on the ground in Ukraine right now?

Mr. HARTLEY. Sir, we do not have combat troops. I mean, it depends on how you define it. We have a defense attache. We have officials from the Pentagon that visit. But I think the simple answer is no.

Mr. YOHO. Mr. Chairman, I yield back. Thank you.

Mr. POE. The gentleman yields back. A couple more questions from the Chair and then I will give the ranking member time if he wishes.

Are the Russians going to give Crimea back, Mr. Hartley?

Mr. HARTLEY. Sir, we are doing everything we can to encourage that.

Mr. POE. Okay. I know we are doing that but are they going to give it back, at the end of the day? Is it going to be part of Ukraine or is it going to be part of Russia?

Mr. HARTLEY. Sir, it is our policy that it remains a part of Ukraine and should be returned to Ukrainian control.

Mr. POE. So you don't know. How about you, Ms. Friedt?

Ms. FRIEDT. I agree with Mr. Hartley.

Mr. POE. Okay. We don't know. The 20 kidnapped election watchers—who kidnapped them?

Mr. HARTLEY. Sir, there were—it was a Vienna Document inspection team. They weren't election observers. It was—the team originally—it was composed of eight Europeans led by the Germans and they had five Ukrainian escorts with them. They were kidnapped by pro-Russia individuals or a pro-Russia group in Eastern Ukraine.

Mr. POE. Okay. What were they doing in Eastern Ukraine? You say they were inspectors of what?

Mr. HARTLEY. They were there under the Vienna Document, sir. All 57 nations that are participating states in the Organization for Security and Cooperation in Europe to include Russia have agreed to a set of measures that are intended to build confidence among the partners—among the participants.

Part one mechanism of that is our inspections that each participating state is obliged to receive a certain number of inspections every year. But they can also offer voluntary inspections.

Mr. POE. So they went over there for inspections of what?

Mr. HARTLEY. They were there to inspect Ukrainian military installations and deployments but also to——

Mr. POE. And they were kidnapped by Russian sympathizers?

Mr. HARTLEY. Correct, sir.

Mr. POE. All right. Last question. Is Europe slow walking sanctions because they are concerned about the fact that many of them are totally dependent on Russia for their energy and that Russia may then just retaliate? Is that one of their concerns about sanctions?

Mr. Meeks asked about the Europeans and their not being too supportive, as we would hope in this. Is that part of the reason or do you know, Mr. Hartley?

Mr. HARTLEY. Both we and the Europeans are looking for ways for sanctions that will maximize the impact on the Russians while minimizing the impact on our own economies and businesses. So it is fair to say that that is a consideration of the Europeans, sir.

Mr. POE. All right. Thank you.

I will yield to the ranking member if he has any more questions.

All right. I want to thank both of our witnesses for their participation and any other questions that any members of the panel have will be put in writing and we would expect a response from you.

Thank you very much for being here. The subcommittee is adjourned.

[Whereupon, at 3:18 p.m., the committee was adjourned.]

APPENDIX

MATERIAL SUBMITTED FOR THE RECORD

JOINT SUBCOMMITTEE HEARING NOTICE
COMMITTEE ON FOREIGN AFFAIRS
U.S. HOUSE OF REPRESENTATIVES
WASHINGTON, DC 20515-6128

Subcommittee on Terrorism, Nonproliferation, and Trade
Ted Poe (R-TX), Chairman

Subcommittee on Europe, Eurasia, and Emerging Threats
Dana Rohrabacher (R-CA), Chairman

TO: MEMBERS OF THE COMMITTEE ON FOREIGN AFFAIRS

You are respectfully requested to attend an OPEN hearing of the Committee on Foreign Affairs, to be held jointly by the Subcommittee on Terrorism, Nonproliferation, and Trade and the Subcommittee on Europe, Eurasia, and Emerging Threats in Room 2172 of the Rayburn House Office Building (and available live via the Committee website at http://www.ForeignAffairs.house.gov):

DATE: Tuesday, April 29, 2014

TIME: 1:30 p.m.

SUBJECT: U.S.-Russia Nuclear Arms Negotiations: Ukraine and Beyond

WITNESSES: Ms. Anita E. Friedt
                       Principal Deputy Assistant Secretary for Nuclear and Strategic Policy
                       Bureau of Arms Control, Verification, and Compliance
                       U.S. Department of State

                       Mr. Brent Hartley
                       Deputy Assistant Secretary
                       Bureau of European and Eurasian Affairs
                       U.S. Department of State

By Direction of the Chairman

The Committee on Foreign Affairs seeks to make its facilities accessible to persons with disabilities. If you are in need of special accommodations, please call 202/225-5021 at least four business days in advance of the event, whenever practicable. Questions with regard to special accommodations in general (including availability of Committee materials in alternative formats and assistive listening devices) may be directed to the Committee.

COMMITTEE ON FOREIGN AFFAIRS

MINUTES OF SUBCOMMITTEE ON ___*Terrorism Nonproliferation and Trade; Europe, Eurasia, and Emerging Threats*___ HEARING

Day___*Tuesday*___Date_____*April 29*_____Room_____*2172*_____

Starting Time ___*1:30 p.m.*___ Ending Time ___*3:18 p.m.*___

Recesses ___*1*___ (*2:04* to *2:31*) (____to ____) (____to ____) (____to ____) (____to ____) (____to ____)

Presiding Member(s)

Chairman Ted Poe

Check all of the following that apply:

Open Session ☑   **Electronically Recorded (taped)** ☑
Executive (closed) Session ☐   **Stenographic Record** ☑
Televised ☑

TITLE OF HEARING:

U.S.-Russia Nuclear Arms Negotiations: Ukraine and Beyond

SUBCOMMITTEE MEMBERS PRESENT:

Reps. Poe, Rohrabacher, Marino, Kinzinger, Cotton, Perry, Yoho, Sherman, Keating, Meeks, Vargas, Schneider, Lowenthal

NON-SUBCOMMITTEE MEMBERS PRESENT: *(Mark with an * if they are not members of full committee.)*

HEARING WITNESSES: Same as meeting notice attached? Yes ☑ No ☐
(If "no", please list below and include title, agency, department, or organization.)

STATEMENTS FOR THE RECORD: *(List any statements submitted for the record.)*

QFR - Rohrabacher

TIME SCHEDULED TO RECONVENE _____
or
TIME ADJOURNED ___*3:18 p.m.*___

_____
Subcommittee Staff Director

Questions for the Record Submitted to
Principal Deputy Assistant Secretary Anita Friedt by
Representative Dana Rohrabacher (#1)
House Committee on Foreign Affairs
April 29, 2014

Question:

In 2012 the Department of Defense released an estimate that China operates up to 1,750 ballistic and cruise missiles of the types banned for Russia and our own country under the INF Treaty. That number is in addition to all their other intercontinental range missiles. What arms control concessions has President Obama elicited from the Chinese Communist Party?

Answer:

The strategic nuclear stockpiles of the United States and Russia account for approximately 90 percent of the world's total.

Through the P5 process and bilateral channels, we have encouraged China to demonstrate transparency and restraint in its nuclear program. We have also encouraged China to work with the other P5 members to carry out the nuclear disarmament commitments undertaken in Article VI of the Nuclear Non-Proliferation Treaty (NPT) and the 2010 NPT Review Conference Final Document Action Plan.

**Questions for the Record Submitted to
Principal Deputy Assistant Secretary Anita Friedt by
Representative Dana Rohrabacher (#2)
House Committee on Foreign Affairs
April 29, 2014**

Question:
Is China's arms buildup a factor in whether or not the United States pursues additional arms control measures with Russia?

Answer:
No, the United States and Russia still possess the world's largest nuclear stockpiles, accounting for approximately 90 percent of the world's total. Although the current situation in Ukraine has significantly undermined mutual trust, no one should forget that even in the darkest days of the Cold War, the United States and Russia found it in our mutual interest to work together on reducing the nuclear threat. A large nuclear arsenal is poorly suited for today's security environment, and we remain open to seek negotiated reductions with Russia covering all nuclear weapons when the conditions are conducive for further steps.

As documented in the annual Department of Defense Report to Congress on Military and Security Developments Involving the People's Republic of China, China has been pursuing a long-term modernization of its strategic nuclear forces. We continue to monitor these developments very closely. The President has made clear that the United States is committed to maintaining strategic stability in U.S.-China relations, and supports dialogue on nuclear affairs aimed at fostering a more stable, resilient, and transparent security relationship with China.

**Questions for the Record Submitted to
Principal Deputy Assistant Secretary Anita Friedt by
Representative Dana Rohrabacher (#3)
House Committee on Foreign Affairs
April 29, 2014**

Question:
Does the State Department think it is wise to pursue further nuclear arms control measures with Russia that leave out Communist China? What message does that send to our partners in Asia?

Answer:
Further bilateral negotiations between the United States and Russia are necessary to achieve additional reductions of the two largest nuclear arsenals to lay the ground work for future multilateral negotiations.

We continue to consult closely with our allies on our nuclear arms control and deterrence policies. Our message is clear, the United States remains fully prepared and capable of defending ourselves and our allies with the full range of capabilities available, including the deterrence provided by our conventional and nuclear forces.

It should also be noted that our Asian allies are supportive of our arms control and nonproliferation efforts in both word and deed.

Questions for the Record Submitted to
Principal Deputy Assistant Secretary Anita Friedt by
Representative Dana Rohrabacher (#4)
House Committee on Foreign Affairs
April 29, 2014

Question:
What efforts has the Administration made to engage China on arms control?
What has the Chinese response been?

Answer:
We have encouraged China through our bilateral engagements and in
P5 engagements to demonstrate transparency and to work to meet its
disarmament commitments. The Chinese have been active participants in
the P5 process and just hosted the most recent meeting in Beijing from April
15-16. China also chairs the Glossary on Nuclear Terms and Definitions
Working Group in the P5 process. This work increases mutual
understanding, facilitates further discussions among the P5 on nuclear
issues, and lays the groundwork for eventual nuclear negotiations that
involve all five NPT nuclear weapon states.
The United States remains committed to maintaining strategic stability
in U.S.-China relations and supports a continued bilateral dialogue aimed at
fostering a more stable, resilient, and transparent security relationship with
China.

Questions for the Record Submitted to
Principal Deputy Assistant Secretary Anita Friedt by
Representative Dana Rohrabacher (#5)
House Committee on Foreign Affairs
April 29, 2014

Question:

Does China's ballistic arms buildup invalidate the administration's belief that arms control is only a bilateral issue for the U.S. and Russia to negotiate?

Answer:

No, the United States and Russia still possess the world's largest nuclear stockpiles, accounting for approximately 90 percent of the world's total. However, we continue to encourage China through the P5 process and other venues to demonstrate transparency and restraint in its nuclear program and to work to advance its nuclear disarmament commitments undertaken in Article VI of the NPT and the 2010 NPT Review Conference Final Document Action Plan.

www.ingramcontent.com/pod-product-compliance
Lightning Source LLC
Chambersburg PA
CBHW081755280526
45789CB00008B/2867